SEASONS

SEASONS

A BOOK OF POEMS

by Charlotte Zolotow

illustrated by Erik Blegvad

HarperCollinsPublishers

Seasons: A Book of Poems
Text copyright © 2002 by Charlotte Zolotow
Illustrations copyright © 2002 by Erik Blegvad
Printed in the U.S.A. All rights reserved.
www.harperchildrens.com
Library of Congress Cataloging-in-Publication Data
Zolotow, Charlotte.
   Seasons: a book of poems / by Charlotte Zolotow ; illustrated by Erik Blegvad.—1st ed.
   p.   cm. — (An I can read book)
ISBN 0-06-026698-8 — ISBN 0-06-026699-6 (lib. bdg.)
   1. Seasons—Juvenile poetry. 2. Nature—Juvenile poetry. 3. Children's poetry,
American. [1. Seasons—Poetry. 2. Nature—Poetry. 3. American poetry.]
I. Blegvad, Erik, ill. II. Title.
PS3549.O63 S43 2001   00-061409
811'.54—dc21

1 2 3 4 5 6 7 8 9 10

First Edition

To Ned Shank, with love

—C.Z.

Contents

WINTER BITS

Soon

Windrushing day
darkened sky.
Soon
the white snow.

First Snow

There is a special kind of quiet

every household knows

we hear it in our sleep

the first night it snows.

11

Me

This is me.

These are ears.

I hear things

the clock ticking in the hall

the step on our stairs

that creaks.

If I were not me

and lived in another house

there would be other things

to hear and see

for I'd be someone else

not me.

Snow at Night

During the night

the world turned white

I wake to dazzling brightness.

Now it's books

and boots

and off to school.

My footprints in the whiteness.

The Cold

Winter time is windy time
white with snow and iced with snow
spiced with snow the wind will blow
winter time is windy time, winter
time!

The Winter Wind

There is a savage wind

a wild wind

a wind of white-topped waves

rising high

under a cold white

winter sky.

Why?

I'm mad at my mother

and she at me.

Why do we fight

people we like—

as me and my mother

mad at each other

today.

A Small Pine Tree

I can see

in our front yard

a small tree

that delights

hung with lights

at Christmas time

but after Christmas day

when the lights are put away

what I really love to see

is our green-needled

small pine tree.

My Shadow

My shadow

keeps me company

as I walk home

that's why

when the sun is out

I'm never quite alone.

My Mother

My mother doesn't always know

what I am thinking

but I can very often tell

what's in her head

by the things

she hasn't said.

Recess

There's a smell of spring
in the city today
a smell of spring today
Inside the school walls
children play
There's a smell of spring today

There's a wind from the river today
a warm winter wind today
the city trees around the school
bend gently in this fresh wind
in this warm wind
in this river wind

There's a smell of spring

in the city today

a smell of spring today

SPRING THINGS

Spring Song

The winter snow melts away

and the air is soft this sunny day

What does this gentle wind sing?

I know! I know!

  Here comes Spring!

Singing Birds

Springtime is growing time in yellow

yellow green and singing birds

rain sun and soft spring winds

Oh springtime is springtime is wingtime

is growing time

warm and yellow

Nightfall

Light drains slowly from the sky

I almost see

things fade away

and then it's dark

the end of day.

Dark

Close your eyes, close your eyes

the clock ticks the night away

dream deep

dream sweet

think of the soft blue springtime skies

tomorrow's on the way.

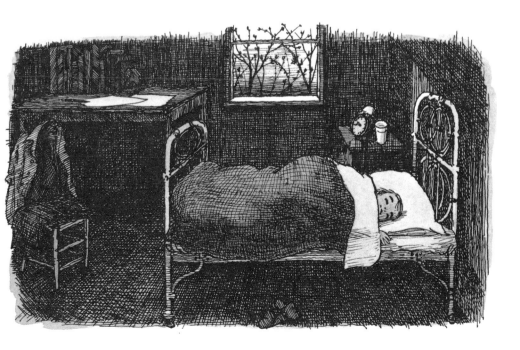

The Spring Wind

There is a wind

light as a feather

against your skin

a soft wind

gentle as a dove.

Spring Rain

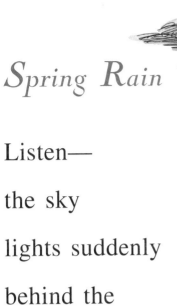

Listen—

the sky

lights suddenly

behind the

dark treetop

and then the

wind

rustles

the leaves

before the rain begins

Indoors

The room is gray

this rainy day

the chairs, the desk

the bed, the rug

and then

rain stops

the room is bright

the chairs, the desk

the bed, the rug

are drowned in yellow light.

The Little Seed

The little seed
that blew here
and tucked into our grass
is not the seed anymore
it's become
OUR SYCAMORE.

My Cat

Furry purry mystery

so soft

so sweet

so graceful

on your white-tipped feet

I wonder what you think

lying next to me

a furry purry lovely

mystery

35

The Tunnel

Streaking along

outside the train

fields and sky

flying by

the train chugs on

down the track

but all at once

all goes black

gone the fields and gone the sky

just the darkness going by

and all I see

is a reflection of me

then suddenly

I disappear

brightness and trees

fields and sky

once again flying by

*O*nion *G*rass

We can taste the wind

with its flavor of wild onion

in our mouths.

We can hear it

moving through the trees

sounding like waves

in the sea.

SUMMER
THOUGHTS

Flowers and Fun

Summertime is sunnytime

funnytime is sunnytime in

summertime

leaves and trees

flowers and fun

summer breeze

but also

beeeezzzzzzzzzz

Spider Web

In the early summer morning

after the rain

small spider

your gray lace web

sparkles with diamonds

of

dew.

Fallen Star

One night I saw

flying low

a little flash of fire

like a star

fallen from the sky.

"Look," my mother said.

"A firefly!"

The Crickets

The crickets
fill the night
with their voices—
It is like
a message
in another language
spoken to a part
of me
who hasn't
happened yet

Anger

First it's dark
then darker still
birds stop singing
everything's still
until . . .

rumbling thunder
tumbles by
flash of lightning
streaks the sky

that's how I feel

when I'm mad at a friend

as though

this loud dark time

will never end

Some Days

It's no fun

days I've done

something mean

sometimes no one knows but me

but I can see

if I'd been a different way

it would have been a better day

for others

and for me.

The Puzzle

So much of every day
it is a mystery
but maybe the puzzle of it
is just me.

Summer Wind

There is a sturdy steady wind

like a little workhorse in the sky.

It turns the blades of windmills

and blows the washing dry.

The Butterfly

Butterfly

flutter by

on your snow white wings

hovering in the summer air

like a song lingering there

you leave an echo sweet and fair

of lullabies

of butterflies

on snow white wings

THE FEEL
OF FALL

Where?

I look up into the sky
and see the birds
like black arrows
flying high.

Where they come from where they go

only they really know

flying flying flying by

in the blueness of the sky.

The Fields of Fall

The world may change

and I'll grow old

but still the fields of fall

will be

gold

filled with fallen leaves

the fields of fall

will be gold

The Fall Wind

There is a strong fresh wind

like an eagle flying by.

It snatches someone's kite

and keeps it flying high.

The Plane

High overhead

on a still fall night

flashing lights of a plane in flight

flying through the darkness

like a lighted torch

while we watch

from our porch

59

Grown-ups

Do mothers ever feel lonely?

Do fathers ever feel sad?

I want mine to be

the way they want me—

happy and glad.

Birthdays

My mother

my mother

flowers for her

she likes them better

than the cake

I prefer

Halloween Night

The moon is full

the night is strange

and filled with mystery

and here are three small ghosts

coming up the walk to me.

Falling Leaves

Autumn time is falling leaves

red and brown, yellow and brown

rustling rustling over the ground

drying stalk and piles of leaves

burning in the wind

smoke and fire

pumpkins and cider

autumn time is falling leaves.

The Birds

The birds call

in the trees

kee keeesheee

for they know

there will soon be rain

then snow!